Hel

Lifelong Friend

by Stephanie Sigue

HOUGHTON MIFFLIN HARCOURT
School Publishers

PHOTOGRAPHY CREDITS: Cover © Bettmann/Corbis; tp © Hulton-Deutsch Collection/Corbis; 3, 5 © Bettmann/Corbis; 7 © Hulton Archive/Getty Images; 9 © Comstock/Corbis; 10 © Hulton-Deutsch Collection/Corbis; 11 © Time & Life Pictures/Getty Images; 12 © Bettmann/Corbis.

Printed in China

ISBN-10: 0-547-25297-8
ISBN-13: 978-0-547-25297-1

15 16 17 18 0940 19 18 17 16
4500569761

Table of Contents

Helen's Early Years

When Helen Keller was born, she was a beautiful, normal baby. There was no reason for her family to believe that she would be any different than any other girl born in 1880.

But when Helen was 19 months old, she became extremely sick. She suffered a high fever. The doctors tried to help her. When Helen finally recovered, she seemed fine. However, her parents soon realized that there had been a huge change.

Helen Keller's illness changed her life.

Helen's illness had left her both deaf and blind. Her mother discovered this when Helen didn't respond to people around her.

By age six, Helen was acting like a wild animal. She threw tantrums. She charged into people, screaming nonstop. She tore things up. She ate with her hands and took food from everyone's plate.

Although her parents showed her affection, Helen left them exhausted. Relatives suggested that the Kellers send Helen to live at a place for other children like her.

Even though Helen was difficult and headstrong, it was clear that she was bright. She used her other senses to identify people and things. Helen's parents searched the country to find a doctor who could cure her. However, they found out that her blindness and deafness could not be reversed.

Help finally came from an unusual source: Alexander Graham Bell, the inventor of the telephone. He suggested that Mr. and Mrs. Keller write to the Perkins Institution in Boston, Massachusetts. There, a young woman, deaf and blind like Helen, had been educated successfully.

Helen's mother wrote to the school's director. He advised the Kellers to hire a young woman, Annie Sullivan, to become Helen's tutor.

Helen Keller (left) with her tutor, Annie Sullivan.

Alexander Graham Bell

Alexander Graham Bell was interested in education for the deaf because both his mother and wife were deaf. He invented techniques of teaching speech to people who were deaf.

Annie Sullivan Meets Helen

Annie met Helen in 1887, just before Helen's seventh birthday. Within a short time, Annie and Helen formed a special bond and would become inseparable. They would go everywhere together until Annie's death, almost 50 years later.

Because Annie had poor eyesight herself, she may have understood Helen better than others. From the beginning, Annie recognized Helen's intelligence. She developed a method of teaching Helen words. She would "spell" a word in Helen's hand using a type of sign language. Then she would have Helen touch the object. Even though Helen learned to spell many words, she didn't understand what they meant.

Helen's family thought some of Annie's methods were harsh, and they often treated her as an intruder. But Annie saw how Helen terrorized her family. She convinced Helen's father to let them live in a cottage on the family's property.

Even when Helen became an adult, Annie (right) remained an important friend and teacher.

Annie moved Helen to the small enclosure, where she was completely separate from everyone else. Although Helen continued to learn quickly, she still didn't understand words and their meanings. One day, Annie held Helen's hand under a water spout and spelled the word *water.* Suddenly, Helen understood that *w-a-t-e-r* and the liquid coming from the spout were the same.

Beyond Alabama

In 1888, Annie and Helen left Alabama. On Helen's first trip away, she and Annie traveled to Boston to meet the students at the Perkins Institution. Helen and Annie spent the next two years at Perkins.

At Perkins, with Annie's help, Helen learned to read lips using her fingers and to read books using Braille. Helen also began to write stories and poems. People learned about her ability to use her hands to talk. Newspapers even started writing articles about her.

When Helen was 11, she had a short story published in a magazine. Little by little, she began to be paid for her writing projects, and she became more well-known.

Perkins Institution

The Perkins Institution, now known as the Perkins School for the Blind, was founded in 1832 by Dr. John Fisher. It is still in operation today in Watertown, Massachusetts. The library at Perkins houses more than 50,000 recorded books and magazines and 16,000 Braille books!

Braille is a system of writing that uses raised dots as symbols for letters. Blind people touch the dots to read the page.

Now Helen was eager for a "real" education. She wanted to go to school, but no school would take a student who was deaf *and* blind. Annie learned of a new school in New York City whose aim was to teach deaf students to speak.

In some ways, while in New York, Helen was like any other student as she attended school, went on field trips, and explored the city. But in other ways, her life was very different. Because Helen was a celebrity, she met many wealthy and famous New Yorkers.

Helen was the first deaf and blind person to earn a college degree.

Off to College

With Annie's encouragement, Helen's education continued. In 1900, she was accepted to Radcliffe College. She was the first deaf and blind person ever to enroll in a college. The class work was extremely difficult. Annie coached and tutored Helen every step of the way. In 1904, Helen graduated.

After graduation, one of Helen's plans was to inform the public about the lives of blind and deaf people and the challenges they face. She began a series of essays that described how she used her senses to understand what was going on around her.

Helen's Causes

Until this time, people didn't know how deaf and blind people felt. Helen's essays made them more aware. In one essay, she wrote about how she could identify a person's age from the vibrations of the person's footsteps. As Helen grew more famous, people from all over the world asked her for help. Helen decided to become a public speaker for the blind.

Annie rarely left Helen's side. She was Helen's voice coach and helped her prepare her speeches. Together, they went on lecture tours. When Helen gave a speech, Annie would give a short introduction, and then Helen would begin.

Helen Keller was determined to help other people.

At their first speech, Helen was terrified, but she adapted quickly. Her audiences loved her. Helen said she used her speeches to encourage people, especially those with disabilities. Although Helen was the star, Annie was the chief figure behind the scenes.

Helen, with Annie's assistance, took up other causes. In New York, she began to write about the divide between the rich and the poor. She wrote about the immigrants and their challenges. Also, she was against segregation, or separation of blacks and whites. She became involved in women's suffrage, which was the movement for women's right to vote.

Many women worked hard for women's rights. In 1920, women were finally given the right to vote.

Helen and Annie's Last Years

Over the years, Helen's writings had been Annie and Helen's means of support. Helen also became a spokesperson for the American Foundation for the Blind. This organization provided information, books, and education for people who were blind.

Although many of Helen's views were considered radical, or extreme, they helped draw attention to the foundation. The two women crisscrossed the country (and later Europe) on fundraising trips, giving speeches and visiting schools for the deaf and blind. Helen even spoke to Congress in support of a bill to provide public libraries for the blind.

It was during this time that Annie became seriously ill. She died in 1936, at 70 years old. Annie Sullivan, whom Helen had always called "Teacher," had been Helen's companion since Helen was six years old.

Helen's Later Years

After Annie's death, Helen continued to travel. During World War II, she visited blind, deaf, and wounded soldiers in hospitals. Afterward, she continued to be an important voice for people with disabilities. Helen Keller's life story became a successful Broadway play, *The Miracle Worker*.

Annie Sullivan was more than Helen Keller's teacher. She unlocked Helen's silent and dark world by helping her communicate. She also remained a life-long companion. Annie taught Helen so much and, by doing so, helped Helen teach the world even more.

Important Dates

- **1880**—Helen is born.
- **1887**—Annie Sullivan begins teaching Helen.
- **1888**—Helen and Annie leave for Perkins.
- **1904**—Helen is the first deaf-blind person to graduate from college.
- **1924**—Helen becomes a fundraiser for the American Foundation for the Blind.
- **1936**—Annie Sullivan dies at age 70.
- **1940–1960s**—Helen travels the world, helping people with disabilities.
- **1968**—Helen Keller dies at age 87.

Responding

TARGET SKILL **Compare and Contrast**

How were Annie Sullivan and Helen Keller similar and different? Compare and contrast the two women. Copy and complete the chart below.

Annie	Both	Helen
With her vision and hearing, Annie could help Helen communicate.	?	?

Write About It

Text to World Write an informative paragraph describing a person you know whose life involved a series of interesting events. Describe these interesting events in detail. Use words such as *first*, *next*, and *finally* to make the order of events clear.

TARGET VOCABULARY

affection	enclosure
bond	exhausted
charged	inseparable
chief	intruder
companion	suffered

TARGET SKILL **Compare and Contrast** Examine how details or ideas are alike or different.

TARGET STRATEGY **Analyze/Evaluate** Think carefully about the text and form an opinion about it.

GENRE **Narrative Nonfiction** gives factual information by telling a true story.